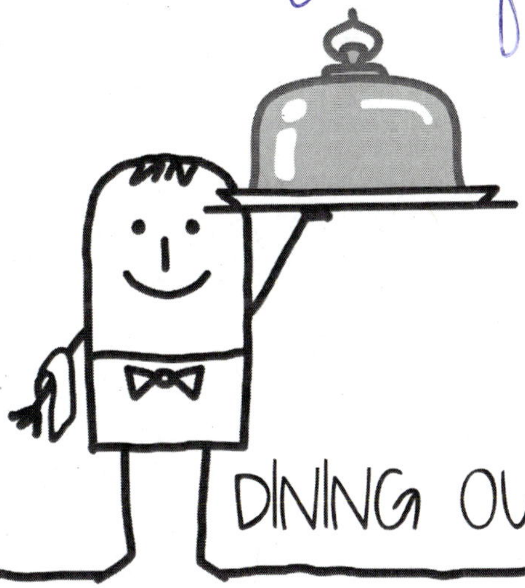

DINING OUT 101

an insider's guide to getting better service in North American restaurants

served up by Jared Hunt & Crystal Stranaghan

Dining Out 101 first published in Canada by CCS-Crystal Clear Solutions, an imprint of Gumboot Books. All rights reserved. No part of this publication may be reproduced or transmitted in any form or by any means, electronic or mechanical, including photocopying, recording or by any information storage and retrieval system now known or to be invented, without permission in writing from the publisher.

ISBN 978-1-926691-23-7

This edition printed and bound in Canada.

text copyright 2011
by Jared Hunt and Crystal Stranaghan

all images © copyright by NLshop and licensed for use through shutterstock.com

acknowledgements

Writing a book is not something that happens in a vacuum. The ongoing support and encouragement from friends, family and colleagues is what keeps us going through the hundreds of hours it takes to get from idea to finished product.

We would like to thank everyone who contributed their suggestions and feedback to this book during the brainstorming, writing, editing and layout stages, especially: Karen, Pete, Darrin, Brian, Katrina, Marnie, Paul, Dave P. and Melanie. And to anyone we have forgotten to name, we apologize. You are appreciated.

Thank you also to all of our guests - the people we served during our employments in various restaurants - for your patience. We hope that others can learn from what you have taught us over the years.

this book is dedicated to everyone who loves food...

table of contents

9 ... INTRODUCTIONS
  12 ... Jared
  14 ... Crystal
  16 ... Some Notes on Layout

17 ... WHERE SHOULD WE GO?
  18 ... Pete, Simon & Sean
  20 ... Research
  22 ... Considerations
  25 ... Types of Restaurants
  31 ... Chain vs. Independent

33 ... MAKING A RESERVATION
  34 ... Dave & Noreen
  37 ... Reservation Basics

41 ... CAST & CREW
  42 ... Bill & the Businessmen
  46 ... What do all these people do?

57 ... PLEASE, HAVE A SEAT
    58 ... Steve & Family
    61 ... Checking Things Out
    64 ... If You Don't Like Your Table
    66 ... If You're In a Hurry

67 ... MAY I TAKE YOUR ORDER?
    68 ... Cory & Sophie
    72 ... The Clubhouse Question
    73 ... The Universal Signal
    74 ... Restrictions
    76 ... Recommendations
    78 ... Modifying The Menu
    79 ... Lost in Translation

81 ... THE MAIN EVENT
    82 ... Christy & Friends
    86 ... Courses
    88 ... Wine
    90 ... How is everything?
    92 ... Lost in Translation
    93 ... When You're Done
    94 ... Lost in Translation

95 ... CHEQUE PLEASE
- 96 ... Karl & Client
- 98 ... Paying For Your Meal
- 99 ... Lost in Translation
- 100 ... Tipping
- 103 ... Automatic Gratuity
- 104 ... Paying Your Bill
- 105 ... The End

107 ... BAD SERVER
- 108 ... Options
- 110 ... Strategies

113 ... IN CONCLUSION
- 115 ... PDF & ePub copies for FREE!

117 ... GLOSSARY

Our original inspiration

for writing this book came from watching people (friends and family as well as strangers) enduring bad restaurant experiences that just didn't need to be so. It was a subject that came up often enough that we started to analyze why it was happening.

One of our first observations was that our friends in the restaurant industry seemed to have fewer really bad experiences than the ones outside the industry, even though they tended to eat out more often. At first glance it seemed like there could be two easy reasons for this:

1. *Industry people get better service.* Our research confirmed what we knew intuitively. Very few people who work in the industry bother to inform the restaurant staff of that fact when they go somewhere to eat. It does happen, but not often enough to account for the overall difference we saw in industry vs. non-industry dining experiences.

2. *Industry people are easier to please.* Anyone with friends who work in restaurants will tell you this is simply not true. If anything, industry people tend to be fussier than people with less knowledge of how restaurants work.

So, there had to be another explanation, and we went looking for it.

What we found is that there is no absolute answer. Each dining experience is unique and, unfortunately, there is no single method for guaranteeing a good one. That being said, our comparison of people working in the restaurant industry with those who don't still proved useful. You can summarize the advantage held by industry people in two words: inside information.

That information contributes to better dining experiences in two big ways:

1. *Choice of location.* People who work in restaurants talk to other people who work in restaurants. They know about the new places and they hear reviews from customers and other staff members. This helps them choose the right restaurant for the right occasion.

2. *Understanding.* Industry people have to endure the same bad service as everyone else, but they're usually not as upset about it because they can see what's causing it. It may be just as annoying, but at least it isn't a mystery, and sometimes steps can be taken to help the situation.

To answer the original question, then, we wrote this book because we wanted you to have access to that inside information. We're convinced that if everyone had a better understanding of how restaurants worked, they'd be able to make better decisions about where to go, and they'd be able to manage both their server and their expectations to get the best possible dining experience.

In our opinion, any experience that results in the customer being upset, disappointed or angry is a bad one. Our intent is to give you as many tools as we can that will empower you as a customer to improve your dining experiences. We can't guarantee that everything will always be perfect, but we're confident that we can make at least a small improvement in every restaurant experience.

Before we go too much further, we'd like to take a minute to introduce ourselves.

I love restaurants.

I love watching different styles of service and I love savouring a new combination of flavours.

I still love restaurants when the service is bad.

I still love restaurants when the food isn't great.

Eating out is a hobby of mine and I do it as often as I can.

I started working in the food and beverage industry when I was 19 years old. My first job was in Room Service at the Waterfront Centre Hotel (now the Fairmont Waterfront), where I spent just over five years (including three as a supervisor). High points during my time in room service included serving Prince William and Prince Harry during their visit to Vancouver, and acting as a coordinator for the department during the Vancouver Asia-Pacific Economic Cooperation (APEC) conference. In addition to my time in Vancouver, I also spent 10 months in Room Service at the Royal York Hotel in Toronto.

After coming back to Vancouver from the Royal York, I spent some time as a host in Griffins Restaurant in the Hotel Vancouver.

My next stop was back at the Waterfront Hotel in Herons Restaurant, where I put in some time as a busser and host before becoming a server again. It was during this time as a fine dining server that I really got into the nuts and bolts of how to create and enjoy a perfect dining experience. The standards we set for ourselves as servers were extremely high and included memorizing the ingredient list and preparation techniques for all items on the dinner menu. I also owe a large portion of my wine knowledge to the sommeliers-in-training I worked with there.

After 10+ years in the hotel and fine dining biz, I decided it was time for something a little more relaxed. My next position was in an upscale pub setting, where I worked for about two-and-a-half years – including during the 2010 Olympics.

My time in the restaurant industry came to an end in the fall of 2010 so that I could focus full-time on my writing career (though I still hear it calling me from time to time).

When I set off on my bike with a résumé in hand, I didn't exactly have a career in the restaurant industry in mind. In fact, at 12 years old, I'd only been in a handful of restaurants in my entire life. But, as luck would have it, the first business I came to was a restaurant called G Willies. I looked older than I was, and at that moment they had a warehouse filled with dirty dishes and a busy restaurant keeping all their existing staff busy. The job was mine.

In the 20 years since then, I have always had a restaurant job of some kind – whether it was in the kitchen, out front serving tables, or behind the bar. I've worked in a vegetarian juice-bar with 10 tables where everything was organic and made from scratch, and I got to make up a new menu every day. I've been a baker in a café that featured my grandmother's cookie recipes and finely crafted espresso drinks; and I've worked in the kitchen of a fancy Italian place that made their own pasta from scratch.

I mastered the art of the hamburger and the ultimate hedgehog milkshake at the Cola Diner to the accompaniment of live jazz music, and learned the finer points of spinning pizza dough (and late-night delivery survival skills) from a pro at a pizza and lobster joint. I've worked the bar and collected glasses in a haunted hotel ballroom on the west coast of Ireland, and served at a bustling nightclub-style bar on Granville Street in downtown Vancouver.

The last six years have seen me happily settled in Vancouver as a server at Steamworks – one of the biggest (seating for over 700 people), and busiest, brewpubs I've ever seen.

People are often shocked when they find out I have several university degrees and spend my time outside the restaurant running a successful consulting firm. "WHY are you still working as a server?" they want to know.

My only answer is this: I don't want to give it up. I like the buzz and the energy, the people and the music, the drinks and the food, and the glimpses I get into people's lives as they come and go around me.

some notes on layout

We've tried to lay out this book in the order of a typical dining experience, starting with deciding where to go, making a reservation, arriving, ordering, enjoying and then paying. We finish off with a glossary of restaurant terms.

Along the way, you will see sections we call *Lost in Translation* that explore some of the common miscommunications we've noticed between restaurant staff and their guests.

Each chapter begins with an anecdote describing a restaurant experience and an analysis of what happened during that experience. The anecdotes are fictional (although based on things we have witnessed and/or experienced). They are mostly for entertainment, but are loosely related to the contents of the chapter they are attached to.

If you enjoy the anecdotes, and/or want to share some of your own, be sure to visit www.diningout101.com. We plan to share more of our own experiences, and we'd love to hear yours!

Pete, Simon and Sean *were all wearing their jerseys as they stomped down the sidewalk toward the pub Pete had spotted the other day. It was an hour 'til game time and they wanted to be sure they had great seats.*

At first glance, the place seemed perfect. The lights were low and there was a huge TV above the bar. The bartender nodded as they entered. "Have a seat wherever," he called out, and slapped three menus on the bar nearby.

Pete grabbed the menus and led Simon and Sean over to a corner booth. No matter which way they turned, they couldn't all look at the same TV, but they didn't think much of it – surely all the TVs would be showing the game, anyway.

A few pints later, Pete started getting concerned. The big TV above the bar wasn't showing the pre-game show yet. He called over their server and asked about it.

"Sorry mate, Man U. vs. Chelsea tonight on the big screen – owner's orders. I can put your game on the closer screen, though." He pointed to the nearest TV.

"Are you kidding me?" said Pete. "What if everyone asks to change it?"

The server laughed. "Good luck with that. All the guys at the bar are here specifically for the football - and I don't mean the NFL."

The three of them let out groans. It was five minutes until kick-off. There was no way they'd get a decent seat anywhere else at this point. Well, maybe they could take turns sitting in the awkward seat craning their necks ...

What went wrong?

This is a pretty clear failure in the research stage. If any of the guys had called ahead, or even asked the bartender when they arrived, they would have had time to scout around for another pub that would be playing the game they wanted to watch.

A critical part of enjoying your dining experience is in your choice of where to go. The decision you make here is the first, and possibly the most important, way you can influence how much you're going to enjoy your upcoming meal.

We refer to this as the research stage. Research is important because, in order to make a good decision, you need to gather good information. To help you gather that good information, the next section will give you an overview of the types of restaurants common in North America. We'll also give you some clues to look for when trying to figure out what kind of restaurant you're looking at.

When analyzing restaurants, we find it helpful to use the three classic categories that form the initials QSA.

Quality: This refers specifically to the quality of the food and beverage on offer.

Service: The knowledge, attitude and timing of the restaurant staff.

Atmosphere: The overall cleanliness and ambience of the restaurant. The best food ever prepared, served by the best server in history, could still be ruined if it was presented in a filthy restaurant next door to a booming nightclub or construction site.

If it's available and convenient, we recommend doing an online search to help you gather information.

Sites such as www.yelp.com (or .ca) rate restaurants based on prices, as well as a variety of other criteria that can be helpful in making your decision.

If someone else is deciding where you'll go to eat, you might still enjoy the next section on Types of Restaurants. Even when you aren't the one making the decision, knowing a bit more about the type of restaurant will help you set your expectations.

Budget

The amount of money you're ready to spend is a natural place to begin when you're choosing a restaurant. The key here is balance. You're weighing your expectations for service, food and atmosphere against the amount you want to pay.

In our opinion, unrealistic expectations at this level are one of the most common reasons for unhappy diners. Taking a moment to really think about what you want for your money will go a long way toward setting up a positive experience.

Type of Event

Closely related to your budget is the occasion you're going out for. You may want to choose a nicer restaurant to celebrate your 10th anniversary than you would to watch a sporting event.

When you're doing your research, try to find out if the restaurant layout and facilities will work with your plans. For example: If you're going out to watch a football game, make sure the restaurant has enough TVs. If you're going out for a celebratory dinner with your spouse, make sure the restaurant can offer a quiet table. If you want to spend some time on your laptop while you enjoy a cup of coffee, then be sure the place offers an Internet connection, and has power outlets available.

Time Available

It is important to take speed of service into account when you're deciding where to go. A gorgeous, lovingly crafted meal presented by a gracious and knowledgeable server at a fine dining restaurant is not going to create a positive experience if you only have 30 minutes to eat.

Party Size

Some restaurants specifically target large groups and have policies and procedures in place to support them. At the other end of the scale are restaurants – typically fine dining that won't accept groups larger than a certain size (often eight but sometimes as low as four). Most restaurants fall into a sort of middle ground where they won't turn away a large group, but they aren't particularly well set up for it, either.

If you're planning an event with a large group (anything involving eight or more people), during your research stage you should ask questions about their capacity and policies for groups. It is increasingly common for restaurants to automatically apply a gratuity to bills on large groups. It is also common for the group to share a single cheque. If you require individual cheques, you should definitely specify when making the reservation (or at least when being seated, before ordering). It's never too late to call ahead – even if you are already on your way, those few extra minutes for the restaurant to prepare may make a world of difference.

Specific questions to ask:

- What size of group can they accommodate?

- Will a gratuity be added automatically?

- Are separate cheques an option?

- Is there a maximum amount of time we can have the table for?

- How will tables for the group be laid out? (Everyone at one long table? Several tables close together? An entire section for the group?)

If you're planning a special event as a couple, you may still want to pay attention to both the policies on large parties and the layout of the restaurant. Large parties can't help but make a little more noise, and being seated near one can impact the tone of a romantic evening.

Types of Restaurants

There seem to be as many different classifications for restaurants as there are restaurant critics and review sites. Some people will disagree with the categories we list here, but the intent is just to provide a common vocabulary for the rest of the book. We'll also provide some clues to look for when you're in a restaurant trying to figure out what category it falls into.

Since the focus of this book is on getting better service, we've decided not to discuss fast-food restaurants and coffee shops. These types of restaurants certainly have their place in the dining landscape, but the level of interaction between guest and staff is usually very low. We can't really help you there, so we're leaving them out of this particular discussion.

Café/Diner

Cafés are usually the lowest-priced restaurants that still offer table service. They are typically not licensed to serve alcohol. In addition to low prices, the advantages of a café tend to be speedy service and free coffee refills. Cafes are usually open late (or even 24 hours) and often offer all-day breakfast. This is not the place to look for cutting-edge cuisine or servers with extensive menu knowledge, though café servers have provided some of the most hospitable and informative experiences in my dining history.

A cafe is an ideal place for a simple breakfast or a quick, cheap, sit-down meal to break up the monotony of a road trip. It's also the ideal place to spend time filling out post-cards, working on your laptop or sending e-mails, as they often have free Internet access and places to plug in your computer.

There is enough cross-over between cafés and diners that we've decided to group them together. A diner will usually be slightly more expensive and they usually have a wider variety of items on the menu, but are otherwise quite similar.

Clues:

- Small, tightly positioned tables; possibly a counter with stools for single diners to sit at.

- No tablecloths or place settings.

- Simple, laminated menus.

- Servers usually wear simple (often very old-fashioned) uniforms.

Pub/Bar

In North America, pubs are usually restaurants with full menus, but they focus on alcoholic beverage sales. This is in contrast to many European pubs where some nuts or a packet of crisps are the only non-alcohol items you'll find. Pub menus focus on comfort food and there tends to be a very high proportion of salty, deep-fried items (to encourage that next drink order).

Pub service tends to focus on getting you your next drink in the most efficient manner possible. However, as long as you're ready for simple fare, meals in a pub can be excellent.

Depending on local licensing guidelines, pubs may or may not be able to accommodate children.

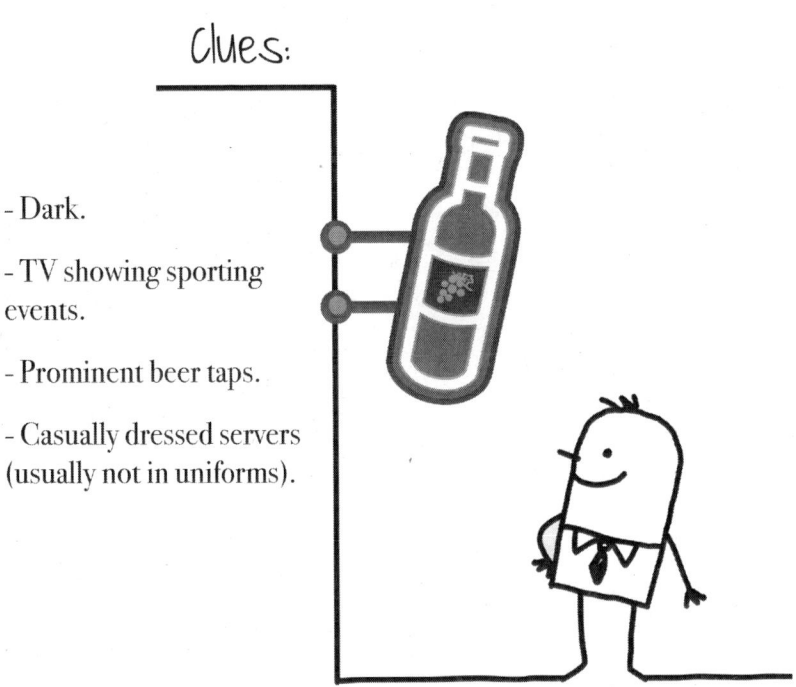

Clues:

- Dark.

- TV showing sporting events.

- Prominent beer taps.

- Casually dressed servers (usually not in uniforms).

Upscale

In-between pub and fine dining is this very large category. Upscale restaurants typically take a diner or pub concept and invest a little more in decor and food presentation. Conversely, an upscale restaurant can also result when a fine dining concept is toned down to make it more widely accessible. Upscale menus usually offer a wide variety of items to try and cater to the widest possible market.

Though there is nothing at all wrong with restaurants in this category, the fact that they occupy a middle ground makes it very difficult to accurately set your expectations. Overall, we've found that upscale restaurants are likely to provide an adequate, but not exceptional, experience for a variety of occasions. Broad appeal is both their strongest advantage and greatest weakness. Many popular chain restaurants fit into this category.

Clues:

- Young, attractive servers.

- Trendy uniforms (or all-black clothing).

- Elaborate floor plans (to maximize seating but provide furniture and plants or other decor items to break up sight lines).

Fine Dining

Fine dining restaurants offer the most involved food presentation, the most polished service and the most expensive ingredients. Their prices are also much higher than those of restaurants from lower tiers. Fine dining menus are often tightly focused on a single style of cuisine, and it is uncommon to find more than 10-15 items to choose from for each course.

Fine dining restaurants are ideal for special occasions. The combination of knowledgeable staff, skillfully-prepared food and elegant atmosphere can make for memorable experiences. That being said, expectations for fine dining are high, and some of the worst experiences we've heard of are a result of restaurants not being able to live up to the hype they've created for themselves.

Clues:

- Formally dressed servers (usually in uniform).

- Quiet.

- Widely spaced tables.

- Finely crafted menus.

- Very high prices.

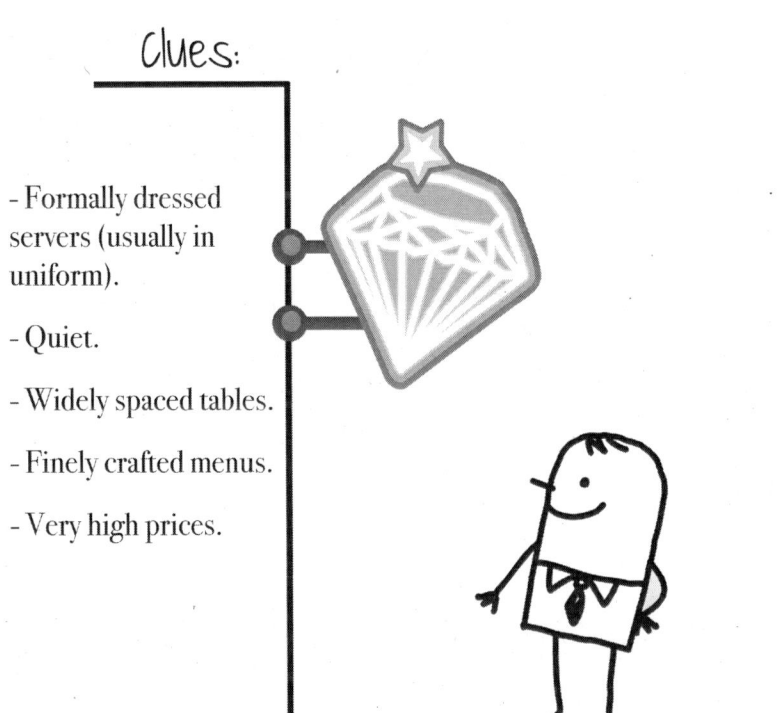

Sub-Categories

In addition to the broad categories, there are some sub-categories to consider.

Ethnic

Restaurants focusing on the cuisine of a specific country or region can fall into any category from diner to fine dining. Most ethnic restaurants in North America adopt Western customs, so you can use the majority of the clues listed above to figure out what category they fit into.

Family

Family restaurants are usually diners or upscale restaurants that have options aimed at children.

When deciding between dining at an independent restaurant or one that is part of a chain, what you're really choosing is whether you value consistency or character. In general, chains are successful because they are able to reproduce a very similar experience for all of their customers. This is reflected in the decor, menu, staff training and service standards. Unique character is one sacrifice that is often made to achieve this consistency. Overall, a chain restaurant is more likely to meet your expectations, but they seldom exceed them.

Dave looked over at Noreen *and congratulated himself on how perfectly his plans for their anniversary were coming together. She was excited to have an occasion to wear her new dress, and they were both happy about getting to try out that fancy new restaurant all their friends were talking about.*

They were lucky enough to find a parking spot nice and close to the restaurant. They walked up to the hostess grinning ear to ear. "Table for two, please," said Dave.

"Do you have a reservation?" asked the pretty young hostess.

Dave hadn't thought to make a reservation on a weeknight. "Uh, no. Is that a problem?"

"Not at all," said the hostess. "I'll have something for you in just a minute."

The minute turned out to be five, but that was nothing compared to the long waits they showed on TV in the New York restaurants, so Dave didn't think much of it. As they followed the hostess to their table, Dave looked around the restaurant and saw several empty tables, including a few right next to the windows.

The hostess led them past all the window tables and finally stopped in front of a table tucked in the far back corner of the restaurant. "Here we are," she said cheerfully, and she pulled out a chair for Noreen.

Dave could see Noreen was disappointed, but she was a good sport and she started to sit down. "Wait," he said, "I don't like this table."

"Oh, I'm sorry," said the hostess. She led them to another table, this one right beside the entrance to the kitchen.

Dave was starting to get a little upset now. "I don't want to sit right beside the kitchen, either," he said.

The hostess looked a bit flustered. "Um, if you could wait here for a moment I'll just check the computer."

Noreen took Dave's hand and squeezed it while giving him a smile. "What is taking so long?" he thought to himself.

When the hostess came back, she brought them to one of the tables by the window. "That's better," said Dave. "Why didn't we just start here?" he added, after the hostess left.

Dave and Noreen watched the man they assumed was their server as he made his way to and from the other six tables around them. He smiled and welcomed them, but it was more than five minutes before he even came over to take their drink order. By that time Dave was downright mad.

And everything had started so well...

What went wrong?

- By not calling ahead to make a reservation, Dave missed a chance to help the restaurant improve the experience. At the least, it would have prevented the five-minute wait when they arrived.

- Dave and Noreen failed to mention that they were out for a special occasion (their anniversary). This could have been done when calling ahead to reserve a table or during their first exchange with the hostess.

- Though it was good that Dave expressed his desire for a different table, he wasn't specific about what he was hoping for. This led to another table he didn't like, which increased his aggravation and flustered the hostess. (It would have been helpful if the hostess had asked, but she didn't.)

- The table they ended up at was in a full section, and the server wasn't ready for them yet, which resulted in a long delay before he could even take their drink orders. In contrast, when she brought them to the first table, the hostess was deliberately putting them in a place where the server was ready to spend some time with them immediately.

Reservation Basics

Once you've decided where to go, the next step is to make a reservation. Our general rule is, if you *can* make a reservation, you should. Some restaurants don't accept them, and that's fine: they'll be set up to deal with walk-ins. Sometimes you're deciding at the last minute. Again, that's okay: if the restaurant can seat you, they will. However, even if it's only an hour in advance, making a reservation is one factor in your control that can help the restaurant make your experience better. Even if it's a place you know doesn't take reservations, they can still give you an idea of whether or not they currently have tables available.

The focus of this chapter is to present you with the information a restaurant will need to make a complete and accurate reservation. Ideally, the person taking your reservation would ask for all of this information, but we've always found it's better not to leave anything to chance.

Time

The first, and most critical, piece of necessary information is the time you'd like to be seated. Be conservative, but precise. Depending on the restaurant, you may or may not lose your reservation if you're late.

Name

Some restaurants have a policy about this, but we've found it's useful to include both first and last names, or your company name if it's a business event. This is especially true if the people in your party will be arriving separately. The more information you can provide, the easier it will be for the restaurant staff to direct you and your guests to the right place.

Phone Number

Most restaurants will not hold a reservation if you can't provide contact information. A cellular phone number is ideal so they can contact you after you've left your home or office.

Party Size

Be as precise as you can. Busy restaurants will have trouble increasing the size of your party at the last minute if extra people show up.

Conversely, if you're planning a larger party, some restaurants have a "minimum spend" based on the number of people on the original reservation. If a large portion of your party doesn't show up, you might get stuck with an additional charge. This isn't a common policy, but it is something we've run into, so it's best to double-check.

Occasions

Most restaurants appreciate knowing if your reservation is for a special occasion. It not only allows them to provide appropriate service, but it may also result in some complimentary items!

Allergies

Especially in the case of severe allergies, letting the restaurant know in advance will give them more time to accommodate you.

Seating Requests

Common seating requests include:

- View.

- Single table or multiple close tables (for larger groups).

- Proximity to kitchen.

- Quiet.

Separate Cheques

As mentioned in the research stage, some restaurants have policies regarding cheques for large parties. If it is important that your group have separate cheques, be sure to ask about it when making the reservation.

CAST & CREW

The meetings *had taken up the entire afternoon, but Bill was happy with the result. The clients had finally accepted his terms and the project would be ready to start on the first of the month. Now that the paperwork was signed, it was time to get out of the office and into the hot new restaurant he had booked a table at.*

Spirits were high. Everyone embraced his suggestion that they walk the four blocks to the restaurant instead of taking separate taxis. Bill's instinct was to spend a little more time soothing the clients' nerves before they went off on their own. This was the biggest deal they had ever signed and he didn't want anyone getting cold feet.

"Thomas Consulting, party of 12?" queried the man at the door when they arrived.

"Crap," thought Bill to himself. The client had shown up with two extra people and Bill had added two junior partners to the meeting, but he hadn't had time to change the reservation. "Yep, that's us," he replied. He'd just get the guy to add another table when they got there.

The guy who brought them in grabbed another staff member and they managed to shift over another nearby table, but it still left four people outside of the main group. Thinking quickly, Bill got everyone on their feet and turned the pre-dinner drinks into a cocktail party where everyone could mill around and chat. It took their server a long time to get everyone matched up with their drinks, but eventually they all had a beverage and the toasts could start.

When they settled down to order dinner, Bill couldn't believe there was only one person serving them. The kid seemed completely flustered. It took him almost 10 minutes to get everyone's orders and he left half the menus sitting on their tables. Bill was so annoyed he forgot to ask for no salt on his meal, but he managed to get the attention of another kid who was wiping down a nearby table, and asked him to pass the instruction on to the server.

When their meals arrived, Bill could plainly see that his steak had salt on it. When he cut into the meat, he saw that, instead of the medium-rare he had ordered, this steak was well-done. He didn't want to make a scene, so he just started eating. A minute later, one of the clients sent back his steak and Bill overheard him ask for it to be cooked more.

"I think you kinda oversold this place, Bill," said another of the clients.

Bill did his best to cover it, but he felt a bit of heat rising under his collar...

What went wrong?

- In a perfect world, restaurants would always be able to adapt when you're forced to change things at the last minute. If the occasion is important, however, it makes sense not to depend on that.

- The first thing Bill could have done is call ahead with the change in numbers. The more notice the better, but even five minutes' notice could have made a big difference in the restaurant's readiness.

- If he had informed the host that numbers had changed when they arrived, the group probably would have had to wait at the front for a few minutes, but the rest of the meal could have proceeded without having to squash tables together awkwardly.

- Very few restaurants are set up to deal with cocktail-party style service (in fact, in regions with strict liquor laws it may actually be illegal). This will often result in a confused server calling out drinks rather than smoothly bringing people exactly what they ordered without fuss. If you are requesting separate cheques, matching drinks with food orders once people are seated can also be much more difficult.

- Depending on the restaurant size, policies, and available support staff, increasing the size of an already large group can result in a server who isn't properly set up to deal with it. In Bill's case, the server definitely needed some back-up, but the restaurant didn't, or wasn't able to, provide it – and Bill's group had to deal with the consequences.

- Particularly if you're part of a large group, always speak directly to your server if you need to modify your order. In Bill's case, he informed a busser instead of his server, and a miscommunication resulted in him getting the wrong meal.

- Even when he saw that his meal was wrong, Bill didn't speak up. If he had, Bill might have been able to simply swap plates with the client who received his medium-rare steak by accident, and no one would have had to wait longer for their meal.

What do all these people **do**?

Have you ever been to a nice restaurant and noticed that there was a different person to: bring you to your table, take your order, open your wine, deliver your food, check to see if you liked it, and then to clear your dishes? Each restaurant has its own unique system for making sure all of those things are done properly. Whether it's all done by the same person or each duty is performed by someone different, understanding the division of labour in a restaurant is an important part of becoming an insider.

Hostess (or Host)

A restaurant hostess has the same goal as the hostess of a party – they do their best to make sure everyone is having a good time. That includes customers, servers, kitchen staff and managers.

More specifically, a restaurant host or hostess is usually responsible for:

- Bringing guests to their tables.

- Providing menus to each guest.

- Monitoring business volume, both in each individual section as well as the restaurant as a whole.

- Handling reservations. This includes gathering the correct information from people making reservations (by phone or Internet) and then assigning those reservations to available tables.

- Payment processing. In restaurants where payment is not handled at table-side, the hostess might be responsible for it. (This will usually be indicated on the bill with a phrase such as Please Pay at the Front or Please Pay Cashier).

The hostess position is often considered a stepping stone toward becoming a server. In other cases, the hostess acts as a supervisor in addition to her other duties.

Identifying

- Positioned near the entrance to the restaurant.

- Often younger.

- Uniform may be slightly more formal than other staff members.

Server

While every staff member in a restaurant is there to help make your experience better, your server is your most direct advocate. They will be your primary contact during your time in the restaurant and, depending on the size and exact policies, your server may be the only person you deal with directly. A server's duties usually include:

- Taking orders (food and beverage, possibly just one or the other) and accurately conveying them to the kitchen and/or bartender.

- Answering questions about items on the menu.

- Making recommendations (may include wine or other beverage pairing with menu items).

- Delivering items (or coordinating their delivery).

- Ensuring guests are enjoying their experience. While Hollywood often portrays servers as bitter and angry enemies of their customers, the truth is that your server is on your side.

- Payment processing. Most North American restaurants handle payment at table-side. (This will usually be indicated on the bill with the phrase Please Pay Your Server.)

A server's focus is on the tables in their section rather than the restaurant as a whole.

Identifying

- Usually the first person to greet you once you're seated.

- Usually wear an apron as part of their uniform.

Bartender

The bartender's primary responsibility is to prepare alcoholic beverages. He is usually responsible for controlling beverage inventory and may or may not also be responsible for handling a cash float or "till."

In restaurants that have a service bar, the bartender is also responsible for serving the guests seated there.

Identifying

- The guy/gal behind the bar.

Busser

Also known as service assistant, or by the less politically-correct title of busboy, a busser's primary function is to keep the restaurant clean and to ensure that empty tables are ready for new guests to be seated. Specifically this includes:

- Clearing glassware and dishes that guests are finished with.

- Cleaning and resetting tables.

- May include filling/refilling water glasses and delivering bread.

Bussing tables is a common rite of passage for people hoping to pursue other jobs in the industry. As such, bussers typically have less experience than other staff members. If you have questions or if you want to place an order, it's usually best to have the busser send your server over, rather than having them pass questions and/or requests along.

Identifying

- Often younger.

- Usually carry a cloth for wiping down tables.

- Might carry a plastic bin for collecting dirty dishes.

- Different-coloured apron (often white).

Expediter

Sometimes called a second server or back server, an expediter's job revolves around delivering food. This usually means answering any questions the kitchen staff have about the orders coming from the servers, coordinating the orders with the food coming from the kitchen, and then making sure all the items arrive at the right tables. Part of the art form involved in food service is to also coordinate things so that all the food arrives at the same time, and that the expediters know which guest ordered what, without having to ask.

While a server focuses on a specific group of tables (their section), expediters are usually responsible for delivering food to the entire restaurant. Therefore, although a good expediter will be quite familiar with the menu, it's usually better to direct your questions to your server. Likewise, an expediter may be able to bring you additional items or modifications, but it's still better to at least check with your server so that they can follow up.

Identifying

- Always carrying plates of food (often on large trays).

Sommelier

Also known as the wine steward, a sommelier's job revolves around wine service. In some restaurants, sommelier is a title (like a degree or diploma) rather than a position. In that case, the sommelier will also have their own section in addition to helping other servers with wine pairings. In higher-end restaurants, the sommelier instead acts as a support server for the entire restaurant, engaging each table in conversation to help figure out which wine each guest would enjoy the most, and what would best complement their food choices.

Sommeliers are usually also responsible for creating, maintaining and rotating the restaurant's wine list. Getting to know your sommelier can be a good way to find out about obscure wines you might otherwise never try (and you may even get special pricing for "bin ends," or wines the restaurant is almost out of).

Identifying

- A sommelier will usually be dressed like the other servers.

- If in doubt, feel free to ask. Most sommeliers are passionate about their field and happy to talk more.

Cook

Though you usually won't get to see them, cooks obviously perform an important function in a restaurant. Beyond just preparing the items on the menu, however, a good restaurant cook is able to coordinate their efforts with the rest of the kitchen staff. Their aim is to have all the items ordered by each table completed at the same time, so that nothing has to sit and wait before it gets delivered.

Chef

In traditional kitchens, there is only one Chef, and the title is used on par with Doctor. That's a lot less common in modern North American kitchens but, if you get a chance to meet the chef, addressing her as Chef is one of those little things that will help you sound like an insider.

Becoming a chef involves years of formal training mixed with practical work experience, which is usually organized along a path from apprentice, to journeyman, and finally to master chef. The difference between a cook and a chef, then, isn't necessarily one of skill or experience – it is usually a reflection of the type of training they have received.

Manager

While providing a great experience for guests is the main job of everyone working in a restaurant, managers have to perform a tricky balancing act involving guest needs, the needs of the staff, and those of the owner or shareholders.

In a perfect world, the manager's job would be to stop by and "touch" each table – that is, welcome each guest and make sure everything is going well. Unfortunately, things don't go perfectly every time, so the manager is responsible for dealing with any issues that come up.

More specifically, Managers deal with:

Food and beverage *Quality* issues

- Temperature.
- Taste.
- Presentation.
- Portion size.
- Price.

Service issues

- Timing.
- Staff attitude.
- Errors.

Atmosphere issues

- Noise.
- Temperature.
- Smells.

Identifying

- Managers are usually dressed more formally than other staff.
- Last name on their name tag.
- Usually older than other staff.

Steve pulled the minivan *off the highway and into the restaurant parking lot. Neither he nor Pam had ever heard of this place before, but they had been on the road for four hours and the kids were starving. Familiar or not, it was the first restaurant they could find and it would have to do.*

Steve couldn't help but notice that every single staff member was young, attractive and dressed in skimpy, all-black clothing. The hostess seated them at a large table and put down five menus. Pam was about to ask for kids' menus, but the hostess had already returned to the front of the restaurant.

By the time the server came over to say hi, the kids were squirming, squealing and poking each other. Apparently the restaurant didn't have apple juice, so Pam ordered orange juice for the kids, a glass of wine for herself and a coke for Steve. The server returned five minutes later with their drinks and asked if they had any questions about the menu.

"Do you have anything for kids?" asked Pam.

The server thought for a moment. "We don't have a kids' menu, but we could probably do a half order of the spaghetti."

"I don't like pisghetti!" said Thomas, smacking his menu on the table and spilling some of his orange juice.

Several arduous minutes later, Pam managed to order a plate of plain pasta noodles with three small bowls for the kids and a chef salad for her. Steve added a burger and fries for himself – at this rate he was going to need something to keep up his strength.

The 20 minutes it took for the food to arrive seemed more like an hour. Pam had finally taken away the kids' orange juice after the third time she'd had to ask for extra napkins to clean up spills.

In the end, the kids got more pasta on the table than they ate. Pam had a bite or two of her salad and asked for the rest to be packed up. Steve got to eat half of his burger, but didn't bother asking for a take-out container. He had a lot more driving to do and, at that point, he didn't really feel like eating, anyway ...

What went wrong?

- The first problem the family encountered was not being able to learn anything about the restaurant before arriving. Ideally they would have been able to choose a restaurant that catered to families.

- Once inside, they were presented with multiple clues that the restaurant wasn't ready for kids (no kids' menus, no booths, skimpy attire on the staff).

- They placed their drink orders separately from their food order, which delayed their food by five-10 minutes. Servers experienced in dealing with children will at least take the kids' food order at the same time as the drinks. If they don't – which is common in restaurants that don't cater to families – it's best to request it. Don't let the server leave the table until they've got the kids' orders!

- Most restaurants default to a tall glass to serve juice and soda for presentation reasons. Ask for a short glass (or rocks glass) with a straw instead, to minimize spillage.

The first few minutes after entering the

restaurant can often set the tone for the entire experience. Among other things, this is a time you can gather some information about what kind of experience to expect – especially if you haven't been to the restaurant before.

This chapter will guide you through the process from entering the restaurant and being seated, up to the point where you're ready to order (which is the subject of the next chapter).

Checking Things Out

Particularly if you're in an unfamiliar restaurant, the time spent walking from the door to your table is a good time to try and figure out exactly what kind of place you're in. If you've done your research, you should have some idea already. In that case, this time can be spent figuring out if the information you gathered was correct.

Business Volume

A full restaurant is usually, but not always, the sign of a good restaurant. A busy room also adds to that ethereal quality we call ambience. Don't assume, however, that an empty restaurant is a bad one. All restaurants have slow times and the failing may actually be one of location or marketing rather than quality.

(It's also worth noting that there are many reasons a sub-par restaurant could be very busy, including location, a special event nearby, or a big conference in town.)

The downside of a full restaurant is that you might have to wait longer for your food and drinks to be prepared and served. If time is a big factor and you've walked into a packed restaurant, you may want to consider another location.

Cleanliness

It's very rare for a restaurant to serve dirty dishes or cutlery (though it does happen accidentally from time to time) but you can tell a lot about the priority placed on cleanliness by looking at other, smaller things as you walk through.

   - Are the menus clean and in good condition?

- Are the staff well-groomed?

- Is the floor swept?

- Are the chairs and tables clean and in good condition?

No matter how cheap the food is, the bare minimum you should expect is a clean chair and tabletop. All the other factors will vary according to the quality of the restaurant. They don't necessarily reflect the quality of food or service, but they do reflect the overall attention to detail.

Table Spacing

Tightly spaced tables indicate that the restaurant is prioritizing profit over comfort and service. On the other hand, too much space between tables can create an empty and cavernous feeling. This is a pretty subjective area, but it's still a piece of the puzzle to consider.

Sight-lines

Another subjective issue is the way a restaurant uses decor to break up sight-lines. The perfect balance is to create a sense of privacy for each table while maintaining the buzz that makes a busy room attractive.

Decor

You can tell a lot about the priorities of a restaurant by checking out the quality and uniformity of tables, chairs, wall-hangings, pictures, windows and paraphernalia used to decorate. Aside from the need to have places for people to sit and eat, everything is an artistic choice. You may or may not appreciate what the designer was trying to do, but you can still make a guess about the owner's attention to detail.

If you don't like your table

You may have noticed that nicer restaurants almost always have a host or hostess available to seat guests, rather than allowing them to seat themselves.

If you're seated by a hostess, they usually have a good reason for taking you to this particular table (and it very rarely has anything to do with whether they like you or not). Among the most common reasons for a hostess choosing a particular table:

- Rotation. Greeting new guests and getting them started usually takes a server several minutes. If a server receives too many tables in too short a period, chances are good that they won't be able to provide their best service. To counter this, the hostess will attempt to give each server one table at a time, rotating through the restaurant to ensure a balance.

- Regulations. Certain areas of a restaurant may only be allowed to serve patrons over the legal drinking age, and only certain areas are suitable if you are only planning to have a drink, and no food.

- Other reservations. In order to make sure they can accommodate everyone, hostesses have to plan out where everyone is going to sit. Though you may pass by tables that are empty at the moment, chances are good that they're reserved for future guests.

- Parties. Depending on the restaurant layout, not all areas can accommodate large groups, and the hostess must take that into account when seating smaller groups.

NOTE: Hollywood seems to have convinced people that restaurant hosts are bitter gatekeepers, desperate for any reason to refuse admission and demanding hefty bribes to secure a decent table. Outside of the very hottest restaurants in New York and Los

Angeles, this is exceptionally rare. Competition in the restaurant industry is fierce and profit margins are low. Most North American restaurants (even the good ones) are in a constant struggle to stay in business. The reality is that if they aren't seating you, it's because they can't, not because they don't want to.

If you're really unhappy with the table you've been brought to, you should speak up. To help make it easier for the hostess to accommodate you, try to be as specific as possible about what you don't like and/or what you're hoping for.

- Proximity to kitchen/entrance/exit?

- View?

- Less noise?

- Privacy?

It's not always possible for the hostess to provide exactly the table you're hoping for but, the more specific you can be, the more likely your needs will be met.

If You're in a Hurry

Communication is the key to speeding up restaurant service. Good servers are careful not to make people feel pressured, and one of the ways they do this is by giving their guests ample time to make decisions. If time is a factor, this low-pressure approach is your enemy. There is no need to be rude, but make sure you let your server know you're in a hurry as soon as you can.

Other things you can do to speed up service:

- Have your drink and food orders ready at the same time, and be sure your whole party is ready to order. North American service typically presents beverages as a separate course at the beginning of the meal. If you'd prefer not to do that, you can usually save several minutes by ordering everything together.

- Ask about quicker prep-time items. Often salads, cold sandwiches, and deep-fried foods can be prepared more quickly. Ask your server if they have any recommendations about items that can be prepared quickly.

- Avoid high-prep time items. Blender drinks (margaritas, piña coladas) are a classic item that simply can't be sped up much, and muddled drinks are close behind (mojitos, old-fashioneds). Similarly, well-done meats have a bare minimum cooking time that can't be sped up without sacrificing taste and presentation.

A glance down the right-hand side of the menu reminded Cory just how expensive this *restaurant was, but he didn't mind, much. The important thing was to make a big impression and, judging by the radiant smile on Sophia's face, he was pretty sure it was working.*

"Last time I was here I had the truffle gnocchi," he said. *"Absolutely amazing."*

"I'm not a big fan of truffles, but I do love gnocchi," replied Sophia.

Before Cory could reply, their server approached the table. "Forgive the interruption," *he said.* "I just wanted to mention our evening's special. Farafalle primavera with snow peas and asparagus in a light cream sauce."

"Oh, that sounds great," said Sophia.

"May I bring you something to drink while you decide on your meals?" asked their server.

Cory ordered the bottle of Shiraz he had chosen based on the fact that it was the third-least expensive red. He didn't want to get "cheap" wine, but he couldn't afford to spend hundreds of dollars, either.

"Certainly, sir," said their server. "Would you be interested in any other recommendations?"

"No, thank you. We'll have the Shiraz."

"Very good, sir."

Cory turned back to Sophia as their server went to get the wine. "So you think you'll have the special?"

"I think so. And maybe a mista salad to start."

"Sounds good."

Their server returned a few minutes later and presented the wine. Cory tasted a bit, approved it, and the server poured for them both. While he was pouring, Sophia placed her order and Cory added a seared-tuna with avocado appetizer and a six-ounce, medium-rare beef tenderloin for himself.

While they were making small talk about work, a different server dropped off two tiny plates for them. "An amuse for you tonight," he said. "Rabbit wrapped in prosciutto with a cabbage and carrot slaw." Sophia's face went pale, but she smiled and thanked him.

"Is everything okay?" asked Cory, after the server left.

"It's just that I'm vegetarian."

"Oh, sorry, I didn't know."

"It's fine. Would you like to have mine? I'm sure it's very tasty." She pushed the tiny plate across the table as if it might infect her.

Cory reached out and took the plate. "It would be a shame to waste it," he said with a wry grin.

Their appetizers arrived shortly after the amuse plates were taken away and Cory tried to keep up the small talk. Sophia seemed like she was enjoying her salad and his tuna was amazing. "What do you think of the wine?" he asked, after he noticed that her glass looked nearly untouched.

"Oh, it's good," she replied. "It just doesn't go that well with the salad."

She had a good point. The tuna was excellent, but he could hardly taste it if he had it with the wine.

That aside, the appetizers were great and they were both delighted by the cucumber-sorbet palate cleanser their server brought out after.

The presentation of their main courses was only outdone by the flavours. Cory's steak was perfectly medium-rare and Sophia raved about her pasta. She mentioned how good it was when their server came back to check on them.

"Oh yes," he replied, "the chef tells me the secret is using chicken stock as a base for the sauce."

Sophia's face turned pale green and she dropped her fork. "I need to use the washroom," she said ...

What went wrong?

- Cory's choice of wine was not bad for his main course, but it clashed with every other item they ordered. The server attempted to make other recommendations but Cory declined.

- As Sophia learned the hard way, many dishes that sound vegetarian have hidden ingredients. Always mention your specific dietary restrictions before you order, whether they're preferences or allergies. Many places can happily offer alternatives, but only if they know in advance.

The Clubhouse Question

One of my favourite ways of evaluating a server is to ask, without even looking at the menu,

"Is your clubhouse chicken or turkey?"

A clubhouse sandwich is one of those items that seems to be on 80 percent or more of all North American restaurant menus, and most restaurants will be able to make one even if it isn't on the menu – assuming they have the ingredients in the kitchen. The server's response to this question will tell you quite a bit.

- If they have to think for a while, or if they don't know the answer, chances are they don't know the menu very well.

- If they point out a clubhouse sandwich on the menu, do they add any commentary? A recommendation or warning? Additional options? This is a good indicator of the server's attitude as well as their menu knowledge.

- If there isn't a clubhouse on the menu, how does the server phrase their response? Did they assure you that the kitchen could prepare one, anyway?

- If they tell you they can't make one, how was their response phrased? This will tell you a bit about your server and it will also let you know how the restaurant handles special requests.

This question won't really work in a lot of ethnic restaurants (though you'd be amazed how many westernized Chinese restaurants have a clubhouse on the menu). It is also a bit limited in very high-end fine dining. That being said, if you're about to spend hundreds of dollars on a meal and you really want that meal to be a clubhouse sandwich, they should be able to accommodate you.

(Don't be too hard on a server who can't answer the clubhouse question. More often than not it will be a result of inexperience or insufficient training rather than bad attitude.)

The Universal Signal

The best way to let your server know that you're ready to order is to close your menu and put it on the table in front of you. You could even take the next step of stacking the menus together on a corner of the table to show you're in a hurry.

We still recommend taking this step even if you still have some questions about the menu. Closed menus are an extremely efficient non-verbal signal that you need some attention. If it's a binder-style menu and you need to refer back to a certain page, mark that page with your finger, or another closed menu, for easy reference.

Restrictions

If you have any dietary restrictions, we recommend letting your server know right away. We also recommend being as specific as possible about the nature of your restrictions.

Depending on how your server did on the clubhouse question, you may want to have them check with the kitchen about any restrictions you're adamant about.

Please keep in mind that kitchen and serving staff will accommodate your special requests as best they can, but try to be patient if your food is taking longer than you'd hoped. Varying from the set menu items often means kitchen staff can't use the items that are stocked and ready. If you have time restrictions, you should try to choose options that are a regular part of the menu, or at the very least ask your server if it will be possible to prepare a special request in the time you have available to you.

Vegetarian

Be specific about how sensitive you are. Many people classify themselves as vegetarians, but will eat fish/seafood (and sometimes poultry as well). It's also good to check about soups and sauces that might seem vegetarian-friendly. There may not actually be pieces of meat in the dish, but it is very common for soups and sauces to have a base of meat stock.

Vegan

Well, if you're vegan, you've probably developed your own coping strategies to deal with the rest of us barbarians. Just be sure you're specific about what vegan means (no mayo, no cheese, no milk, etc.) if your server looks a little confused when you inform them.

Allergies

Be very specific about what you can and can't have. Because of the severity of some allergies, restaurants tend to overreact and may rule out most of the menu. On the other hand, if your allergy really is severe, it's best not to guess and take your chances about whether an item will be okay. Once again, if your server failed the clubhouse question, feel free to ask that they check directly with the kitchen before making your final selection.

Be sure to inform your server if it is a "contact" allergy (for example, if someone touches a prawn and then your plate, your throat will swell shut) as this will allow the kitchen to take extra precautions. Many people with a number of allergies find it helpful to have business-type cards printed with a list of what they can't have. If you give one of your cards to your server, they can submit it to the kitchen with your order for easy reference.

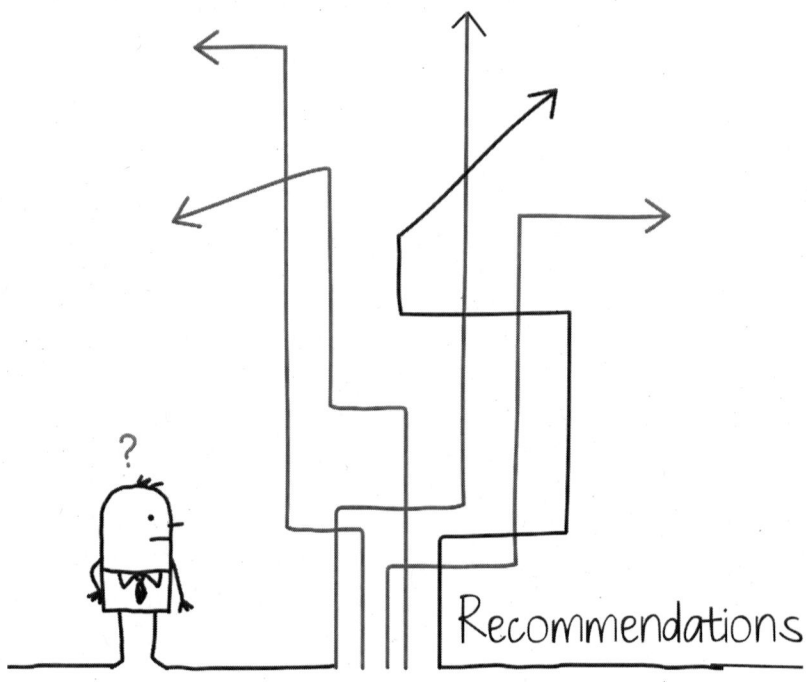

It may not be universal, but among the servers I know, the worst possible question a guest can ask is:

"What do you have that's good?"

The problems with this question are many and varied, but the main problem is that it's non-specific. Good is a completely relative term and the information you get back is very unlikely to be helpful.

I suspect this question originally served the same purpose as our clubhouse question. It isn't being asked for the sake of the answer's content; it's a quick way of evaluating the server and restaurant. The reason we recommend against it is that it's too easy to answer with, "Everything!"

A slightly better, but still not great, question is:

"What's your favourite?"

Or:

"What's the best thing on the menu?"

These are slightly better because they're more specific. However, they are still very arbitrary and will only give you useful information if your tastes are the same as your server's.

Asking, "What is your most popular dish?" is not a bad question, assuming you're willing to order based on popular opinion.

"Is there a house specialty?" is pretty good as well, since many restaurants do have a dish they consider the best reflection of the chef's style.

The best questions, however, involve you providing some information that the server can use to give you a meaningful answer. Some examples:

"I feel like having _____. Can you recommend anything with that in it?"

"I have the following restrictions _____. Can you help me find something I can eat?"

"Last time I was here I had _____ and I loved it/ didn't like it. Is there something you can recommend?"

Assuming your server passed the clubhouse question, giving her some information to work with will make it much more likely that her answers will help you find a meal you'll enjoy.

Note that if you ask a server about a specific item and they recommend something else instead of answering, it probably means they don't think you'll enjoy it, but aren't allowed to say outright that it's not very good. You'll probably want to order something else.

Modifying the Menu

Every restaurant will have its own policy on ordering things that aren't on the menu (or modifying things that are). Most will allow at least some modifications, but there are a few things you should keep in mind when asking for them.

Timing

A combination of pre-shift preparation and practice allows the chefs to cook menu items quite quickly. Anything that isn't on the menu will lose the benefit of one or both of those factors, and will likely take longer. If time is a factor in your meal, you might want to stick with the menu.

Quality

Any chef worthy of the name can take available ingredients and re-combine them to create a dish a guest is requesting. But there is a reason TV shows feature chefs doing that - it's really hard to do well! When designing a menu, the chef carefully balances cooking time, seasoning, preparation techniques and ingredients to try and create the best-tasting items he can. Those items are taste-tested by multiple people and refined until they are just right. Modifying or creating new menu items takes away the chef's planning advantage, and you may have to accept an item that isn't perfect.

We don't want to completely discourage anyone from ordering the exact dish they want (particularly if you have severe dietary restrictions), but we want you to be aware of how it could impact your overall experience.

Lost in Translation

There are some phrases we hear constantly in the restaurant industry that seem to mean different things to servers and patrons.

When you say...

"We're not ready yet."

Your server hears...

"Leave us alone. We'll call you when we need you."

When you say...

"We're still waiting for some people."

Your server hears...

"Go away until the rest of our party arrives."

In a busy restaurant, you should assume that the server will need to check in with all his other tables before coming back, which will typically take about five minutes. Especially if you're hungry or in a hurry, be as specific about how much time you'd like before the server returns.

Christy and her four best friends *practically ran up to the hostess stand, giggling the whole way.* "We made a reservation," *Tanya said.* "It's under 'Christy's Birthday Party.'"

The hostess glanced down at her screen and smiled. "Party of 12?"

"That's us!"

"We've got your table ready. Follow me."

The restaurant was busy, which wasn't surprising for a Friday night. The girls did a little scouting as they followed the hostess. Their table was great – near the back but not so far that it felt isolated.

"Our friends should be here soon," *said Tanya to the hostess.*

"No problem, we'll bring them in as they arrive," *she replied.*

Four more did arrive a few minutes later: Tanya's boyfriend Jason and three of his friends.

Their server came over to introduce herself just as the guys sat down. "Can I grab drinks for anyone?" *she asked.*

"No, thanks, we're just waiting for some more people," *said Christy.*

"Okay, I'll check in with you later."

They had been chatting for about 10 minutes when Tanya finally asked, "What time are the rest of them supposed to be here?"

"Uh, Carla can't make it," said Jason.

"And Ryan and Kelly got in a fight so they aren't coming, either," added Steve.

"So, who are we waiting for?" asked Christy.

Everyone looked around and laughed. "No one, I guess," said Tanya.

They spent the next five minutes trying to get their server's attention. "Is there anything I can get for you?" she asked, when she finally came over.

"Oh, I don't know; we're in a restaurant. Maybe some drinks and some food?" said Ryan sarcastically.

Their server smiled, but Christy could see she was annoyed. "Sorry, I thought you were waiting for the rest of your group. What can I get you?"

"Yeah, sorry, the other people aren't coming anymore," said Christy.

They each ordered a drink and Ryan ordered a couple of appetizer plates for everyone to share. After writing down their orders, their server walked to the end of the table and grabbed one of the empty chairs.

"Can we just use the seats for our coats and stuff?" said Tanya.

The server nodded and put the chair back in place without a word.

"She's in a bad mood," said Ryan.

The guys spent the rest of the meal joking around and teasing the server every time she came to the table. At one point the manager came over to see how everything was going. They weren't trying to get the girl in trouble, so no one said anything.

"We should hurry up. We're going to be late for the movie!" said Tanya, as their server was clearing away the last of their plates.

"I can bring your cheque right away, if you like," said their server.

"Yes, please," said Christy.

When their cheque arrived, Tanya grabbed it before Christy could. "You can't pay," she said, "It's your birthday!" Everyone huddled around the open billfold, whispering and pointing. After a minute of discussion, Tanya called over their server. "We need to have this split up," she said, and proceeded to list off the items that she had ordered. "Oh, and we'll need the appetizer plates split five ways," she added.

Their server looked a bit bewildered, but she scribbled down a few things on her notepad and took the billfold with her. She came back a few minutes later, looking even more distressed. "I'm sorry," she said, "I can't split things up that many ways. I didn't realize you needed separate cheques."

"Fine, we'll figure it out for ourselves," said Tanya, taking the billfold from the girl's hand.

It took another ten minutes to get everyone's totals sorted out and paid. By the time it was done, everyone was annoyed with everyone else. The icing on the cake came when Ryan was signing the slip for his credit card and noticed that there was a 17 percent gratuity included. They were already running so late they didn't want to deal with it now, but Tanya said she would definitely be calling back tomorrow ...

What went wrong?

- The initial problem was miscommunication between the people coming to the party. This resulted in too many seats at the table (frustrating for the server), and a long wait before anyone placed their orders (frustrating for the guests).

- Ryan made a sarcastic remark to the server. While it was unprofessional of the server to react poorly, she did, and the service she provided was not as good as it would have been. In this case, Ryan's comment was also unwarranted, as the server had been following their instructions (they told her they wanted to wait for the rest of their group).

- No one asked about separate cheques. Depending on the system the restaurant uses and the skill of the server, this can range from an easy fix to nearly impossible to accomplish. If your group needs separate cheques, always ask in advance – if possible before you even order your first item. Also be aware that the computer systems most often keep cheques separate based on where you are seated. If you've asked for separate cheques and you move to a different seat, be sure to tell your server.

- Most North American restaurants automatically add a gratuity to large groups (six or more people). The server and/or the hostess taking the reservation should mention it, but they sometimes forget. Often the person making the reservation is notified, but they won't necessarily notify the others in the party (in this case, Christy forgot to tell her friends because she never saw the bill). If there is any doubt, make sure you ask! It will save lots of time and hard feelings for everyone.

Courses

Here are a few of the courses you might experience in a North American restaurant. (Amuse bouche and intermezzo are generally associated with fine dining.)

Amuse Bouche

Roughly translated as "happy mouth," an amuse bouche is a small portion served before the other courses. This course differs from most in that it is usually not selected by the guest. Instead, the chef chooses ingredients she believes will pair well with the other items that have been ordered and/or will showcase the talents of kitchen.

Appetizer

Also known as a *first course* or *starter*, the appetizer course can serve a number of purposes:

- Get your stomach ready for a larger portion to come.

- Allow you to sample something else from the menu without having to commit to a large portion.

- Make sure you get enough food to be satisfied with your meal.

In North America it's customary to order your main course at the same time as your appetizer, but, if time isn't a factor, it can be fun to order and enjoy your appetizer first and make a decision about your main when you've whetted your appetite.

Intermezzo

Also known as a *palate cleanser*, intermezzo usually comes in the form of a small dish of lightly-flavoured sorbet (cucumber, lemon and mint are all common). This is another course that is usually selected by the chef rather than being ordered by the guest.

Main Course

Many North American menus use the term entrée to refer to the main course, which is strange when you consider that the word translates to "entry" and usually indicates a first course in European restaurants! There are a number of theories about why this is, but we only mention it here for the sake of our European readers who might otherwise be puzzled about why these crazy North Americans think a large steak qualifies as a first course.

Cheese

The purpose of this course is to let you try another group of flavours before you move on to dessert. This works especially well if you still have some wine left from your main course.

NOTE: It doesn't have to be cheese! Any appetizer-sized dish could make a good cheese-course option.

Dessert

Following in the European tradition, North Americans like to conclude a meal with something sweet. One difference is that North American restaurants usually offer after-dinner drinks (such as coffee, tea or liqueur) along with dessert rather than after. Be sure to speak up if you prefer to enjoy them separately.

Wine

Though it isn't quite as prevalent as in European restaurants, pairing wine with food is still a common tradition in North America. If you have chosen to enjoy some wine with your meal, there are a few simple tips that will allow you to not only enjoy the wine more, but will also help you look more like an insider.

Cork

- Don't smell it. It is virtually impossible to accurately judge anything about a wine by the smell of the cork (especially if the winery has adopted the current trend toward plastic corks).

- Assuming your server presents you with a real wooden cork, feel free to pick it up and take a look. If it's falling apart and/or clearly rotten, the wine may still be okay, but this is a warning sign.

- Give it a quick squeeze. A real wooden cork that is very soft and/or wet more than three-quarters of the way through may indicate a problem in the way the wine was stored.

Swirl

- With the wine glass still on the table, grasp the stem as close to the bottom as you can and move it quickly in a circle.

Wine doesn't reach its true flavour until it has mixed with air. Swirling the first small amount is a way of quickly infusing it with air to more accurately simulate the way it will taste once it has been sitting in your glass for a while.

Smell

- The idea is to get your nostrils as close to the wine as possible (without actually touching it). It may help to tilt the glass slightly while smelling.

- Another side effect of swirling is to release the aroma of the wine. To get the best results, smell the wine as quickly as possible after swirling.

At this point you're looking for very strong smells. Cork and vinegar are the classic signs of a wine that has gone off, but very strong smells of any kind may indicate a problem.

Taste

- Take just enough wine to cover your tongue and swish it around your mouth to get a good sense of its flavour.

Assuming you picked the wine, at this point you're really just checking to see if it's spoiled (though most restaurants will allow you to send back a wine if you really don't like it). Thanks to modern bottling techniques, less than one bottle in one thousand spoils before opening.

North American servers are trained to interact with their guests fairly often. In fact, the number of times a server stops at the table is a major way North American diners determine how good the service is. This can seem strange to guests from cultures where servers only approach the table when called for. Rest assured, when your server comes to your table without being called, they aren't assuming that you're unhappy; they just want to make sure you have everything you need to enjoy your meal.

Servers take note: "How is everything?" is a terrible question. It is so overused that it just sends the message that you don't actually care and that your "quality check" is not at all genuine. Great servers ask specific questions related to their guests and the items they have ordered.

In a busy restaurant, unless your server can clearly see you've got a problem, they'll probably fall back on the catch-all question rather than stopping to engage in a more meaningful conversation. Even if they don't ask the perfect question, however, if anything about your meal is not meeting your expectations, now is the best time to speak up!

Remember, our purpose in writing this book is to empower you to make a difference in how much you enjoy your restaurant experience. Providing honest feedback to your server, while there is still time to do something about it, is one of the easiest and most often overlooked ways you can have some control over your enjoyment.

I can't tell you how many times I heard from guests as I was clearing away their empty plates that they really didn't enjoy something about their meal. I've even had someone tell me they were pretty sure they ordered a different item but they ate this one, anyway. I couldn't help but wonder why they didn't mention it any of the two or three times I checked with them during their meal. The most likely answer is that they didn't want to be a bother.

The key point of this section is that you aren't a bother. Your server is on your side, and they want to do what they can to make your experience better.

Whether it's a specific question about the item you've ordered, or the generic "How is everything?" you're doing both yourself and the restaurant a favour by answering honestly. Give them a chance to make it right. They almost always will. If your hesitation comes from not wanting to wait another 20 minutes for your food to be remade, speak up anyway and ask how long it might take to remake the dish. You may be surprised how quickly things can happen for you when you speak up.

Though your server may or may not specifically ask, this is also the time to ask for anything you'd like to add to your meal.

A few helpful phrasings:

- "Thanks for asking. My steak actually appears to be well done and I was hoping for medium."

- "When you have a moment, could you bring the extra sauce for my pasta?"

- "My salad could use a little more dressing. Do you have some available?"

- "This dish is a bit more salty than I can handle. Would it be possible to have it prepared with less salt?"

There is no need to be rude or aggressive when providing your feedback. The restaurant will usually do its best to accommodate your requests regardless of the way you phrase them, but rudeness puts everyone on the defensive and makes it much more difficult to communicate.

When you say:

"Everything is fine."

Your server hears:

"Everything is fine."

Lost in Translation

If everything isn't actually fine, you need to speak up now so we can impress you with how quickly we can take steps to fix the problem!

When You're Done

In North American restaurants, the near-universal signal that you're finished with your meal is to place your cutlery side-by-side on your plate. If you do this, a well-trained server will attempt to take your plate away, even if you still have food remaining. If you just want to rest your cutlery on your plate, perhaps while telling a story, be sure to keep your cutlery spread apart to avoid sending the wrong message.

Other signals that you're done your meal include placing your napkin on your plate or simply pushing your plate toward the middle of the table.

It is common in North America to clear away plates as they are emptied, rather than waiting until all guests are finished. This isn't an indication that your server wants to rush you; they are just trying to be efficient.

Lost in Translation

When you say:

"Not right now." Or, "We're good for now."

Your server hears:

"We're enjoying everything at the moment. We will probably want something else later, so don't bring us a cheque yet."

If you're ready for the cheque, or if there is anything else you need, be sure to let your server know.

When you say:

"No thanks, I think that's all for today."

"We're ready to wrap it up here."

"I think we're all done, thanks."

"No thanks, we're all finished."

"We're all done. Just the cheque (or bill) please."

Your server hears:

"There's nothing else we want. We are ready to leave, so please bring us the cheque."

Karl was starting to get a little anxious. *He and his client had been standing in line in front of the restaurant for nearly 10 minutes. It was lunchtime on a Friday, so he expected the restaurant to be busy, but he had never waited quite this long before.*

Just as he was running out of ideas for small talk, the hostess finally called his name and led them to a table.

"It may not be the healthiest choice, but the burger here is one of the best I've ever had," said Karl after they settled in.

His client looked up and closed the menu he had just opened. "Sold," he said, with a smile.

Karl chuckled and closed his menu, as well.

Their server noticed their closed menus and approached. "Welcome, gentlemen. Let me tell you about our specials." Before Karl could say a word, the server launched into a detailed description of four items that weren't on the menu. "Can I bring you anything to drink while you're deciding?" concluded the server.

"I'll just have a coffee and a water," said Karl.

"The same for me," added his client.

"Great. I'll be right back."

"Oh, I guess we could have ordered," said Karl as their server walked away. "Well, let's get down to business while we wait."

They had just started getting into preliminary details when their server returned with their drinks. He took a minute to compliment them on their choices and gave a detailed explanation of the cooking techniques that made their burger so good. He showed his enthusiasm several more times during the meal, each time taking up a few of the precious minutes Karl had allocated for the lunch meeting.

When he came back to talk about dessert, Karl finally interrupted him. "We're actually trying to have a meeting. Could you give us some privacy for a while?"

"Of course, sir. Sorry to disturb you."

True to his word, their server left them alone. Unfortunately, he was still nowhere to be found when Karl was ready to pay the bill.

After 10 minutes of waiting, Karl finally got up and found a manager, who was able to process his payment.

What went wrong?

- Most of this situation was a result of an overly enthusiastic server. This normally wouldn't be a big deal, but in this case, Karl should have mentioned right away that they were having a meeting so that their server could treat them accordingly.

- When Karl finally interrupted the server, he should have asked for the bill to avoid further delays when he and his client were ready to leave.

- The initial long wait at the door could also have been minimized by calling ahead to make a reservation.

Paying For Your Meal

There are a few things about the process of paying for your meal that may be different in North America.

For one, you probably will not receive a cheque until you specifically ask for it. On the other hand, if you've finished your meal and have declined an offer of any further items, your server will likely interpret this to mean that you're finished and they may bring your cheque.

From a server's perspective, bringing a cheque can be a delicate process.

- If they inquire about payment or drop off the cheque too soon, you may feel rushed, or that your server is asking you to leave.

- If you're ready for your cheque and they don't drop it off, you may feel annoyed at the delay.

To get around the North American taboo about asking for payment, servers often use the question, "Is there anything else I can bring for you?" This generic question is a good time for you as a guest to either request more food or drink, or, if you're ready, to directly ask for the cheque.

Some restaurants have policies about presenting your cheque – often while you are still eating (especially during breakfast service). These policies are in place for the convenience of diners who are in a hurry. If this happens, and you are not in a hurry, you are still welcome to order more items and there is no need to rush.

When your server asks:

"*Can I get you some change?*"

You hear:

"*Do I get to keep it all as a tip?*"

What your server means:

"*I can't see anything sticking out of that billfold and it's still in the same place I put it down on the table. Are you ready to pay yet or should I come back?*"

If you aren't ready to pay yet, you simply have to say, "Sorry, we're not quite ready yet," or, "We need another minute to sort it all out." They'll come back. It's a good idea to give a timeline if you can. "Please come back in a minute," or, "Please come back in a few minutes."

When you say:

"*It's fine.*"

Your server hears:

"*Keep the change.*"

Lost in Translation

Tipping

Gratuities are a sensitive topic in the North American restaurant scene. Guests from elsewhere in the world generally have their own customs, and the interaction can be awkward. Here are a few things to be aware of:

- Restaurant wages in North America are based on servers receiving gratuities. In many states and provinces there is a separate wage for servers that can be as low as $2.13 per hour (some US states). These servers are quite literally living on the tips you provide.

- Food prices in North America reflect the lower wages paid to the employees. As expensive as it might already seem, eating out would be even more expensive if restaurant owners had to cover the cost of higher wages.

- The server only keeps a portion of the tip you provide. Every restaurant has its own policies, but it is common for up to half of the server's tips to go into a pool to be shared with support staff. This may include managers, chefs, bussers, dishwashers, bartenders and/or hostesses. Additionally, the amount of money a server is required to add to the pool is usually based on their total sales during their shift, not on the total of the tips they made. It is possible that the server may have to put more money into the tip pool than the amount of the tip, and the difference has to come from their other earnings.

With those factors in mind, our guidelines for tipping are as follows:

Begin with a base of 15 percent of the bill (before taxes).

If everything met your expectations, 15 percent is a reasonable total. By this we mean:

- The items you ordered were delivered accurately and in a reasonable time.

- If there were any problems, the staff dealt with them quickly, efficiently and politely.

-Your server was polite and efficient.

If you were unhappy with some parts of the experience, it is reasonable to reduce your tip to 10 per cent. By this we mean:

- You expressed concerns about your experience and efforts were made to accommodate you, but the restaurant wasn't able to fix the problem.

-Your server was not as attentive, friendly or accurate as you would have preferred.

If you were completely unhappy with the experience, you may feel like leaving no tip at all, and we understand this. However, we might suggest still leaving five percent, as this small amount will actually express your disappointment better than not tipping at all. We only recommend doing this is cases where:

- You expressed concerns and were either not acknowledged or no effort was made to accommodate you.

- Your server was openly and deliberately rude.

If part of the experience exceeded your expectations, increasing your tip to 20 percent is a nice way of saying thank you. By this we mean:

- The server was able to anticipate and provide for some of your needs without being asked.

- The server was able to provide additional information about part of your meal that helped you to make a better decision and/or to enjoy the meal more.

- If any concerns were expressed, the server ensured you were accommodated and then added something extra to make up for the inconvenience.

Tips of greater than 20 percent are a very generous way to express your gratitude for truly exceptional service.

-Providing travel information and directions or recommendations of what to see on your visit to the area.

-Entertaining your children throughout the process, and assistance with cleaning up after an exceptionally messy meal.

Automatic Gratuity

In some countries, gratuities are automatically added to every bill. Unless you are with a large party, this is not common practice in North American restaurants. In places where it is the policy, it will generally be printed right on the menu, or at the very least your party will either have been informed when they made their reservation, or upon arrival at the restaurant if the hostess is aware you are part of a large group.

If you are not sure if a gratuity has already been added, we recommend a closer look at your bill.

Confusion can often result from our fondness for using initials for the various taxes that may be added to bills for food and alcohol (HST does not stand for host!), but we can assure you that the government receives that money, not your server.

If you see the words TIP, AUTO GRAT, GRAT, GRATUITY or SERVICE as one of the line items on your bill, then that means a gratuity has already been included. This may range from 15-20 percent depending on the restaurant's policy, but will usually be clearly stated on the bill.

If you feel that the service you received truly does not merit a tip of that amount, you should ask to speak with a manager, explain why you feel that way, and ask if they will change the amount of the gratuity on the bill to whatever percentage you feel is appropriate.

Paying Your Bill

Most restaurants in North America will have you pay your server directly. Follow the tips below and your server will guide you through the process.

If you are paying with cash and do not need change, you can simply place your money in the billfold or on the tray provided and hand it to your server. If you are in a busy restaurant or outside on a patio, it is a good policy not to leave cash on your table. It may go astray before your server receives it.

If you are paying with cash and you need change, you can let your server know by placing the cash either on top of the billfold, or so that it sticks out the end of the billfold where it is easily visible. This will indicate you need your server's assistance before you're ready to leave.

If you are planning to pay by credit or debit card, you can leave your card sitting on top of the billfold or tray provided where it is visible to the server, or leave it sticking out the end of the billfold. In many cases, there will be a specific pocket that reads, *Please place card here*, ensuring it sticks out where the server can see it.

If you are with a large group and have requested separate cheques, make sure you begin the payment process with ample time before you need to leave. It may take your server several minutes to get all the separate cheques prepared, printed and handed out to the appropriate people, and even longer to process payment if everyone is paying with credit cards or requires change. It is also helpful to be sure that everyone in your group is ready to pay. If the server has to come back to your table several separate times, you may find yourself unnecessarily running behind.

The End

Unless you specifically agreed otherwise before you were seated, you are under no obligation to leave immediately after paying. If the restaurant is full and others are waiting for a table, it is considered polite to vacate your table so other guests can use it, but don't feel pressured to rush, especially if you are still enjoying food or beverage from your meal.

One happy compromise if you did agree to vacate your table by a certain time, but are not yet ready to leave, is to ask if there is a lounge or bar area where you and your party can move to. Most restaurants are happy to accommodate such a request, and it will definitely go far in making you appear to be an insider.

The unfortunate reality is that sometimes you will get a bad server. Not everyone is in the restaurant industry because they want to be (or should be), and occasionally you as a guest are the one who has to suffer the consequences. If you feel that this is happening to you, there are a few options.

Options

Ask for a manager.

Your first step should be to speak to someone besides the server you're having difficulty with. Be specific about your concerns and be as positive as you can. Keep in mind that a manager's job is to be an advocate for both you and her staff, so angry and aggressive behaviour is unlikely to result in a positive change. If you are certain you want a new server, be specific about it. A manager's instinct may be to give the server more support or to give you a complimentary item, instead of making the change you were really hoping for.

Request to be seated in a different section.

You can avoid making any kind of personal remarks to or about your server by asking for a different table. Ideally, ask for a table that is as far as possible from the one you have now. This will increase your odds of receiving a new server. If there is a hostess, you can ask to sit in someone else's section. She will likely understand what you mean and do her best to accommodate you.

Leave.

It's not the best solution, or the first we recommend, but if you truly believe the service you're receiving will ruin your experience, you have the right to leave. Just be sure to pay for anything you have already consumed, and if possible explain to a manager what has happened so the problems may be addressed.

Manage your server.

If you can identify the problem your server is having, you can take steps to manage your interaction with them. The next section will give you some tips on how to do this.

Strategies

Using your new insider knowledge to manage a server you're unhappy with is the ultimate form of empowered dining – you are taking control of what could otherwise be a poor experience and turning it into a positive one.

Here are a few of the most common problems you might have with a server and some things you can do to manage them.

Disorganized

A server who forgets things can be managed by being organized yourself.

- Ensure everyone is completely ready before you begin ordering.

- Encourage the members of your party to place their orders in sequence around the table.

Slow

Slow service is often not directly the fault of the server. The bar may be unexpectedly busy, causing your drinks to take a while; your server may have had several tables arrive at the same time; or the kitchen may be dealing with a large party that ordered right before you. Regardless, you can compensate for slow service by maximizing the time while the server is with you.

- Communicate that you're in a hurry.

- Have your whole party place their orders at the same time.

- Follow the suggestions in the "If You're in a Hurry" section.

Inaccurate

You can compensate for a server who makes mistakes with your order using the tips for a disorganized server. You can also:

- Request that they write your order down (if they aren't already).

- Write the order down yourself.

NOTE: Both these tips are mostly intended for large groups and are fairly certain to insult the server. However, if you've been experiencing problems with the service you're receiving, you're justified in taking the steps you believe are necessary to enjoy your meal.

Inattentive

The tips that apply to a slow server can be applied to an inattentive one, as well. In addition, you might try casually mentioning that you'll be ordering frequently and would appreciate them stopping by often.

We hope that the insider knowledge we've shared empowers you to impact your future dining experiences in a positive way.

If you find you have questions, or come across things you think should be added to future editions of this book, we would love to hear from you.

Please visit us online at **www.diningout101.com** to see what else we have to offer, and to share your dining out experiences!

Sincerely,

Jared Hunt & Crystal Stranaghan

We greatly appreciate you buying our book,

and we want to make sure that you can access the information in it wherever you go, in whatever format you want it.

If you bought a print copy of this book, we would like to give you a digital package containing pdf (in colour!) and e-pub versions of our book so that you can read them on whatever devices you'd like.

All you have to do is email a photo of yourself holding your print copy to ebooks@diningout101.com and we'll reply to the email with the digital files attached.

PDF & e-PUB copies for FREE!

Insider Lingo Lessons

Some terms and definitions so you can speak the language used in restaurants like an insider...

Autograt: Short form of automatic gratuity, this means that the gratuity (or tip) has already been included on your bill. It will be listed as GRAT, SERVICE, AUTOGRAT, GRATUITY or some variation as a line item on your bill if this is the case.

Allergy: When a person has a negative health consequence due to eating a particular type food (these can range in seriousness from discomfort to death).

Bar: See listing for Pub.

Bartender: The bartender's primary responsibility is to prepare alcoholic beverages. May serve guests at the bar or at tables as well.

Bill: See listing for Cheque

Bin Ends: As part of inventory management, when a specific wine is no longer available (or the sommelier does not intend to order more), restaurants will sometimes offer special prices on the remaining bottles they have in stock.

Busser: Also known as service assistant, or by the less politically-correct title of busboy, a busser's primary function is to keep the restaurant clean and to ensure that empty tables are ready for new guests to be seated.

Cafe: Cafés are usually the lowest-priced restaurants that still offer table service. They are typically not licensed to serve alcohol.

Chain Restaurant: Restaurants with many locations that reproduce a very similar experience for all of their customers across locations.

Chef: In traditional kitchens, there is only one Chef, and the title is used on par with Doctor. They are responsible for running the kitchen, developing menus and supervising all matters of food creation and preparation.

Cheque/Check: The paper that itemizes everything you had during your visit to the restaurant, and shows you how much you need to pay for your meal.

Clubhouse Sandwich: Traditionally, a club sandwich, also called a clubhouse sandwich or double-decker, is a sandwich with two layers of fillings between 3 slices of toasted bread. It is often cut into quarters and held together by hors d'œuvre sticks. There are as many variations as there are restaurants, but the key ingredients tend to be: bacon, turkey/chicken, tomato, lettuce and mayonnaise. Some also include cheese.

Cook(s): Person(s) who prepare all the food items on the menu.

Cover: Restaurant-speak for a guest. Used when talking about business volumes. For example: "We did 100 covers tonight," means the restaurant served 100 guests.

Decor: The physical things that make up the restaurant environment. How the room is "decorated" to make it functional and pleasing to the eye and create the desired mood and atmosphere.

Drink List: The menu that lists cocktails, hard liquor and other beverages the restaurant has to offer. Sometimes this will also list wines.

Ethnic Restaurants: Restaurants focusing on the cuisine of a specific country or region that can fall into any category from diner to fine dining.

Expediter: Sometimes called a second server or back server, an expediter's job revolves around delivering food. This usually means answering any questions the kitchen staff have about the orders coming from the servers, coordinating the orders with the food coming from the kitchen, and then making sure all the items arrive at the right tables.

Family Restaurants: Family restaurants are usually diners or upscale restaurants that have options aimed at children.

Fine Dining: Often focused on a single type of cuisine, Fine dining restaurants offer the most involved food presentation, the most polished service and the most expensive ingredients.

Gratuity: Also called a tip, or service charge, this is a social custom of leaving money in addition to the amount of the bill that is for the server to keep (usually shared with other staff). Generally ranges from 10-20% of the bill before taxes for restaurant staff in North America.

Guest: Modern restaurant-speak term that can be used interchangeably with customer or patron.

Host/Hostess: Generally the first person you meet when you arrive at a restaurant - their job often includes: assigning tables, distributing menus, helping you make any special arrangements with your table and handling reservations.

How is everything?: A generic question used by many servers. It is intended to include: Are you enjoying your meal? Is your food prepared the way you were hoping? Can I bring anything else for you?

Independent Restaurant: A restaurant that does not belong to a larger chain, and usually reflects a more unique and individual style.

Is there anything else I can bring?: Another generic question usually used by a server at the end of a meal to get around the North American taboo about asking for payment.

Manager: Managers have to balance guest needs, the needs of the staff, and those of the owner or shareholders. They deal with food and beverage quality issues, service issues, and atmosphere issues.

Menu: The list (or *card* for our European friends) that shows you what the restaurant has to offer.

Minimum spend: Though it isn't common, some restaurants require guests to spend a minimum amount. This is usually a policy for groups that are taking up a large section of the restaurant. This policy protects the restaurant from potential losses caused by a big group of people who only order a few items.

Muddled drink: Muddling refers to the process of crushing a solid food item such as mint leaves (in the case of a mojito) or mixed fruit (in the case of an old-fashioned) in the bottom of a glass or shaker as part of preparing a cocktail. The intent is to release the flavours of the food items into the beverage.

Pub: In North America, pubs are usually restaurants with full menus, but they focus on alcoholic beverage sales.

QSA: Short for Quality, Service and Atmosphere, this term is used when there is a problem with something in one of the three categories and a manager is removing an item from the customer's bill to compensate for that problem.

Reservation: Arranging ahead of time (by phone, online or in person) for a specific date and time when you will arrive at the restaurant to be sure that the restaurant saves a table for you.

Seat Number: A very common method for keeping track of what each guest has ordered is to assign a constant number to each seat at each table. The server then assigns the items each guest orders according to the seat they are sitting in. This is good to keep in mind if you're hoping for separate cheques. If you've moved from your original seat, you might want to let your server know to make sure your items go with you.

Section: Most restaurants divide their seating area into discrete sections. Each server is responsible for their own section. Typically, one server cannot directly order items for guests in another section (for accountability reasons). It is therefore usually better to ask for your server to be sent over rather than ordering from another employee.

Separate Cheques: The practice of dividing up the total of a restaurant bill according to which patron ordered which item. In cases where this service isn't available, time involved is often the reason. Settlement typically takes one minute per person and the server can't perform other duties. Fifteen people could mean leaving other tables for 15 minutes. How would you feel if you wanted another drink, but had to wait 15 minutes for your server to come back? Alternatively, the computer system used to calculate cheques simply may not have this option in some smaller establishments.

Server: The staff member who is your primary contact during your time in the restaurant and will generally co-ordinate ordering, food deliver, drink delivery and payment.

Service Bar: Refers to a bar that has seats for patrons to sit at and be served directly by the bartender, as opposed to a bar designed to prepare beverages for staff members to deliver.

Short Rocks Glass: Generally a short, wide based glass used to serve mixed drinks in. What we recommend asking for kids beverages in!

Sight-line: This is anything you can see from where you are seated/standing.

Sommelier: Also known as the wine steward, a sommelier's job revolves around wine service. Sommeliers are usually also responsible for creating, maintaining and rotating the restaurant's wine list.

Table Service: Refers to the practice of having restaurant employees take orders and deliver food to the guests' tables rather than having guests order and/or pick up their food.

Tip: See listing for Gratuity.

Tip-pool: Tip money collected from all the servers (amount is usually based on their sales) which is then shared with other staff: bussers, expediters, hostesses, bartenders, kitchen staff etc.

Upscale Restaurant: In-between pub and fine dining, Upscale restaurants typically take a diner or pub concept and invest a little more in decor and food presentation.

Vegan: A person who does not eat any animal products.

Vegetarian: Generally speaking, this is a person who does not eat meat. Definitions vary, as some vegetarians will eat seafood.

Walk-in: Restaurant speak for anyone who does not have a reservation, but simple "walks in" off the street looking for a table.

Wine List: Some restaurants will have a separate wine list - a specific menu showing what wines they have to offer.